# DRAMAST

GW00731366

**GRAHAM STOATE**
*Tavistock School and
Community College,
Devon
Formerly Head of Drama,
Purbeck School,
Wareham, Dorset*

*Cartoons by*
**IAN HARRIS**

Nelson

Thomas Nelson and Sons Ltd
Nelson House    Mayfield Road
Walton-on-Thames    Surrey
KT12 5PL    UK

51 York Place
Edinburgh
EH1 3JD    UK

Thomas Nelson (Hong Kong) Ltd
Toppan Building 10/F
22A Westlands Road
Quarry Bay    Hong Kong

Thomas Nelson Australia
102 Dodds Street
South Melbourne
Victoria 3205    Australia

Nelson Canada
1120 Birchmount Road
Scarborough Ontario
M1K 5G4    Canada

© Graham Stoate 1984
First published by Harrap Limited 1984
(under ISBN 0-245-54065-2)

First published by Thomas Nelson and Sons Ltd 1985

ISBN 0-17-444115-0
NPN 9 8

Printed in Hong Kong.

# CONTENTS

# INTRODUCTION

*Dramastarters* is a collection of over two hundred practical ideas for drama games, exercises and improvisations, which have been tried and tested over a number of years with groups of pupils and adults aged from 7 upwards.

The book was devised in response to the hard-pressed teacher or the reluctant novice to drama looking for solid, practical ideas which *work*. It is hoped that the valid skills which these games and exercises undoubtedly promote, such as group co-operation, physical control, and oral/aural competence, will be evident. Beside each game there is an indication of its purpose or function within the drama lesson, together with a useful list of equipment needed, if any.

## HOW TO PLAN A LESSON USING *DRAMASTARTERS*

Although a monotonously regular programme can be counter-productive, I have found that a recognisably structured lesson can be beneficial for pupils and teacher alike. Good classroom management and control can often be achieved when pupils are presented with the security of a lesson plan which does not vary tremendously from week to week. They can see the acquisition of drama skills as a progressive process. Pupils soon become accustomed to the gradually increasing demands made of them and to the growing self-control they need to exercise as a consequence. Quite quickly, the transition from one activity to another within drama lessons becomes easy, untroubled and natural.

In my own teaching, I find it useful to begin each sixty-minute lesson in the same way. The group is encouraged to change quickly into jeans/teeshirts/plimsolls, and, having done so, to sit on the floor in a large circle for registration. This focus-point is meant to emphasise the break from the rest of the school day which a drama lesson often represents. Gone are the constraints of desks and the more traditional forms of learning:

a new and rather different type of learning has begun.

To underline this, I start most drama lessons with five minutes or so of lively physical activity (see section A), followed by five or ten minutes' quieter more concentrated work (see section B). Then we spend five or ten minutes with a game promoting speech (see section C). This precedes the main activity of each lesson which may be a more extended period of improvisation, lasting about thirty minutes (see section D). I always try to allow some time at the end of the lesson for relaxation (see section B) or discussion, easing pupils back into a frame of mind where they are ready to move on to their next lesson of the school day.

Section E of this book contains suggestions for a complete lesson programme based on this system. It assumes that pupils, and possibly teachers, are inexperienced practitioners of drama, and it attempts to offer a definite sense of progression in the demands these activities make, both in terms of difficulty and control. It also attempts a gradual building of group relationships from solo to pair to whole-group work.

I recognise that lesson plans devised by an outsider can never hope to be the most successful. Group leaders will quickly become skilful in selecting and arranging their own lesson programme based on the ideas offered in *Dramastarters*, to suit both their own teaching/leadership style, and the strengths and weaknesses of their students.

Apart from being of direct use in drama lessons, many of the games and exercises in *Dramastarters* are also relevant to English teachers and can be profitably and easily used in the classroom as well as in the drama studio. They are also intended for use by youth workers and in youth clubs generally.

Graham Stoate

# A LIVELY OPENERS

*A lively, perhaps quite brief, period of physical activity at the
start of every drama lesson has two possible benefits. It can
allow participants to 'let off some steam' or it can invigorate
and enliven them. Either way, it provides a positive focus-
point at the beginning of the lesson.*

## A1 FISHING

**EQUIPMENT**   One chair for each participant
**AIMS**   Physical exercise/control; listening/response; group
participation

Group sits on chairs in a circle, facing *outwards*. Each person is
given the name of a fish, e.g., Cod, Haddock, Plaice, Mackerel.
Usually four species of fish are enough, so that whole group is
sub-divided into four 'fish-groups' around the circle. Leader then
instructs whole group that when s/he shouts the name of a fish,
participants around the circle who have been given that name
should get up from their chairs and run round the outside of the
circle in a clockwise direction until they reach their chair again,
when they should sit down. The last one back is out. For
example: 'Cod!' – all Cods run round circle, last 'Cod' to sit
down is out.

**A2**   **VARIATION**   Call out more than one species at a time –
swimming in shoals! No bumping or elbowing. Good physical
control required here!

**A3**   **VARIATION**   Introduce the concept of tides. Leader may call
'Tide change' when fish are in 'mid-swim'. At this command,
any fish swimming must change direction and run the other
way back to his or her chair.

## A4  JUMP FOR YOUR LIFE!

**EQUIPMENT**  Length of skipping-rope with a bean-bag tied to one end

**AIMS**  Physical exercise/control; group participation

This can be a demanding game for the leader also! Whole group stands in a circle, facing inwards with Leader standing in the centre. Leader rotates a length of skipping rope (about 360cm (12′) radius) on to the end of which is tied a bean bag. Group must jump to avoid the rope. Those who touch it are out.

## A5  VARIATION ˙ Get the group to close their eyes, and/or hold hands.

*'Perhaps I should aim to improve **my** physical co-ordination.'*

8

## A6    TO THE LIFEBOATS!

**EQUIPMENT**  None
**AIMS**  Physical exercise/control; quickness of
response/alertness; group participation; listening

Leader is Captain of a large vessel for which s/he should invent
a name. S/he should first point out the various parts of the ship:
*Port, Starboard, Forward, Aft,* and explain that whenever s/he
shouts 'Port!', for example, the group should run to Port at the
double. Last to reach that area is out. Rapid repetition of several
areas obviously confuses the group and produces lively
movement as members of the group try to get there quickly.

A7  **VARIATION**  Add other captain's orders. For example,
'Captain's inspection!' (all freeze and salute); 'Enemy Aircraft!'
(all fall flat on deck); 'Man overboard!' (all stand on one leg,
shade eyes with one hand); 'Scrub the decks!' etc. – anything to
add to the lively confusion this game engenders!

## A8    STEEPLECHASE

**EQUIPMENT**  None
**AIMS**  Listening/quickness of response/alertness; physical
control; group co-operation and identity

Leader divides whole group into two equal teams. Get two teams
to line up side-by-side, each team member 60cm (2') behind the
next team member. Then get the two teams to face inwards, so
that each person faces the equivalent in the opposing team.
Instruct both teams to sit down on the floor, legs out in front of
them, so that each person's feet touch the feet of the opposing
team member. Give each person a consecutive number. Count
from one end in the first team, and from the other in the second
team. When Leader shouts one of the numbers, the participant
holding that number has to get up and steeplechase over the
members of his or her team who are below him or her in

numerical order, towards the team member holding number 1. (If number 1 is called, s/he should begin at this point.) The steeplechaser can then run to the other end of his or her team and begin 'steeplechasing' back down to his or her place. Upon reaching it, s/he should sit down. First 'steeplechaser' to sit down scores a point for his or her team. Leader should stress that care and control is needed when steeplechasing. Any treading on the unfortunate seated team members should be heavily penalised.

## A9  SIT-DOWN SLALOM

**EQUIPMENT**  Enough chairs for six per team
**AIMS**  Group participation/involvement; physical exercise/control

Leader divides whole group into teams of six or seven. Each team should stand in a line at one end of the room. Arranged in front of each team is a straight line of six chairs facing the team, spaced at 90cm (3′) intervals. The first member of each team must, on the word 'Go!', run *backwards* to the first chair and *without moving it* sit down on it. S/he then moves on, slalom fashion and backwards, to the next chair, repeating the process, until all the chairs have been sat upon. The team member then races *backwards* to join his or her team, and the next member of the group begins. The winning team finishes first. If anyone moves a chair in sitting on it, they must begin their slalom again. Careful adjudication is obviously needed here!

## A10  VARIATION  Do the slalom hopping on one leg.

## A11  DESERT ISLANDS

**EQUIPMENT**  Several spotlights or some chalk
**PREPARATION**  Set up lighting so that there are three or four

pools of light in the studio or draw three or four circles on the floor in chalk
**AIMS**   Quickness of response; mixing of the group; group co-operation

Play some music and get whole group to move around to it. When music plays, the participants should avoid moving into the circles. (If lights are used, be careful that participants do not cast a shadow into the pool of light as well.) Anyone transgressing is out! When music stops whole group must make for an 'island'. Last one there is out!

**A12**   **VARIATION**   Turn out occasionally one of the pools of light, or gradually reduce the number of islands to one by rubbing out the chalk circles.

## A13   TOUCH AND FREEZE

**EQUIPMENT**   None
**AIMS**   Group involvement; alertness; quickness of response; physical control

One of the group volunteers to sit in the centre of the room on the floor. The rest of the group must gather around the volunteer, and stand with one finger touching some part of his or her anatomy. When Leader shouts 'Touch and freeze!' whole group has to move quickly away from the seated volunteer before s/he can tag them. The volunteer cannot move along the ground away from his or her original seated position, and can only reach out to tag on the command 'touch and freeze'. At all other times the volunteer must sit inert. Those tagged sit down next to the volunteer, and the rest of the group move back to the original standing position, with one finger touching one of those seated. The whole process is repeated until every member of the group has been tagged.

## A14  WHACKO!

EQUIPMENT   A (thin) rolled newspaper
AIMS   Alertness/quickness of response; self-control/discipline;
physical control

Whole group sits in a large circle. Each person in the circle is
given a number, consecutively. A rolled newspaper is then
placed in the centre of the circle. Leader calls out a number at
random, say number 10, and Participant 10 runs from the circle
into the centre and picks up the newspaper. Leader then calls a
second number, say 12, and Participant 12 begins to make a
clockwise circuit outside the circle. Participant 10 can leave the
circle at any point and intercept Participant 12, who must
continue to run in a clockwise direction. Participant 10 must
then attempt to chase Participant 12 back to 12's place, giving
him or her a whack with the newspaper, only stopping when 12
finally sits down. No whacking above waist height. This
exercises self-control greatly!


## A15  ON THE BALL

EQUIPMENT   Tennis ball or small object
AIMS   Alertness; quickness of response; physical
exercise/control

Whole group sits in a large circle, and is numbered
consecutively. A tennis ball or other small object is placed in the
centre. Leader calls out two numbers and then shouts 'Fire!' The
participant who holds the first number must get up quickly and
make a clockwise circuit outside the circle, and the participant
who holds the second number must get up and make an anti-
clockwise circuit of the circle. Each enters the circle through the
gap where s/he had been sitting, and each makes a dive to get
the ball or object first.

*'I thought we were supposed to hold it at arm's length.'*

## A16 CATCH THE STICK

**EQUIPMENT** A stick or broomhandle about 150cm (5′) long
**AIMS** Alertness/quickness of response

Whole group sits in a circle, and is numbered consecutively.
Leader stands in centre with a tall stick, held vertically next to
him or her. Leader calls out two numbers, followed by 'Go!', at
which point s/he releases the stick. The two participants holding
the numbers called have to make a dive to catch the stick before
it falls to the ground. The one who is successful can remain in
the centre to support the stick for the next two contestants.

13

## A17  TARGET PRACTICE

**EQUIPMENT**  One plastic football
**AIMS**  Physical control; group participation

Whole group stands in a large circle, facing *outwards*, legs apart.
A volunteer stands in the centre of the circle. One of the group
is given a plastic football. S/he must attempt to roll the ball
under his or her legs, aiming at the person in the centre, who
can only take avoiding action by jumping upwards, not
sideways. If it hits below the knee, the participant in the centre
is out. The ball should be kept in play as much as possible by
every member of the circle.

## A18  HUMAN TUG OF WAR

**EQUIPMENT**  None
**AIMS**  Physical contact; physical control; pair involvement

Leader divides whole group into pairs. Partners should stand
back-to-back, with both feet apart. Participants reach down
between their legs and grasp the hands of their partner. On the
word 'Pull!' each partner tries to pull the other in the direction
they are facing. The winner is the one who pulls the other to a
given point.

*TEAM GAMES are always popular and valuable lively openers, but
try these variations on a theme for a change.*

## A19  THE UNDRESSING GAME

**EQUIPMENT**  For each team – one chair; one old handbag; one
hat; one scarf
**AIMS**  Group co-operation and involvement; lively physical
activity

Leader divides whole group into equal teams. Place an old

handbag, a long woolly scarf, and a hat on a chair at the other end of the room opposite each team. Team Member 1 runs up, puts on the clothing, picks up handbag, and runs back, transfers everything to 2 who takes it back up and leaves it all on the chair. Team Member 3 then runs up to the chair and so on.

## A20 MRS BROWN'S SHOPPING LIST

**EQUIPMENT** None
**AIMS** Listening; alertness; quickness of response; group involvement

Leader divides whole group into teams of six, standing in parallel lines at one end of the room. Give the first member of each team the name 'Butter', the second – 'Sugar', the third – 'Eggs', fourth – 'Tea', fifth – 'Milk', sixth – 'Bread'. Leader tells group that whenever a team member hears his or her 'name' in the story which the Leader is about to tell, s/he has to run to the other end of the room and back to his or her team. For example, if 'Tea' appears in the story, all those who have been given the name 'Tea' have to compete in the relay. If the words 'Shopping list' appear in the story *every* member of every team has to race. Points are scored each time for first one back. Here is the story. Obviously there will be a pause after each key word until the relay is over and points have been scored.

'Another rainy day was dawning as Mrs Brown made her way downstairs. "Oh dear," she murmured to herself, "it's raining. It would be the day I had chosen to go shopping." So she made herself a nice cup of *tea* to cheer herself up, putting in several lumps of *sugar* for good measure. "I'd better have two *eggs* today," she said, as she took in the *milk* bottles which the *milk*man had left for her. "Oh dear, he's forgotten to leave me any *bread*, I'll have to add that to my *shopping list.*" There on the table, right next to the *butter* dish was her *shopping list*. "I'd better check to see if I've got everything down. Let me see . . .

*Butter, sugar, eggs, tea*, . . . I must add *bread* which the *milk*man forgot." After she had finished her breakfast, she left the house, clutching her *shopping list*, and caught the bus to the supermarket, where she quickly found the refrigerated counter. Here she could see lots of margarine, yoghurt, and what seemed like hundreds of cartons of *milk*, but no *butter*. "I definitely need *butter*," she said, "Auntie Ethel doesn't like marg. and I want to make her a nice *bread* and *butter* pudding for *tea*. Ah, here it is. Now is there anything left on my *shopping list*? Let me see . . . *milk, butter, sugar, tea, bread, eggs*. . . . No it's all here." So she made her way to the check out and checked her change *eggs*actly, then threw away her *shopping list* before making her way home once more.'

## OTHER TEAM GAMES

**A21**   Try hopping on the left foot backwards!

**A22**   Carrying the smallest (or largest!) member of the team.

**A23**   Team members stand with legs apart and roll a ball down the line to the back of the team through the legs. Team member at the back retrieves the ball and brings it to the front.

## A24   CHAIN GANG

**EQUIPMENT**   None
**AIMS**   Physical contact; group co-operation and involvement

Leader divides whole group into two teams – some might wish to segregate boys from girls. Teams should line up side-by-side, one team member behind the other, making sure there is plenty of room behind the last participant in each team. Leader tells everyone to stand comfortably with legs apart, then to lean forward placing their *left* arm between their legs and with their *right* hand to grasp the *left* hand of the person in *front*. The object of the game is for each team to travel backwards. The participant at the front begins moving backwards: Participant 2 can move under 1's legs, then stand up. Both 1 and 2 can then edge over 3, who should wait until 1, then 2, have made their way over him or her, at which point 3 can join them in their journey to the back of the team, and so on. No-one should break hand-hold at any time. When 1 has reached the back, and the whole position of the team has been reversed, the whole process can be repeated with 1 making his or her way back to the front of the team again.

## A25  MAD DOG

**EQUIPMENT**   A piece of cloth for each team
**AIMS**   Lively physical activity; group involvement

Leader divides whole group into two or three sub-groups of around 10–12. Participants should stand in straight lines each with his or her arms round the waist of the person in front. The last participant in each line must tuck a handkerchief or piece of cloth into his or her belt. On the word 'Go' from the leader the participant at the front of each team must begin 'chasing their tail', and must try to snatch the piece of cloth from the person at the back. When successful, the participant at the front transfers to the back, and the game recommences with a new head and a new tail for the mad dog!

## A26  TAKE A DEEP BREATH

**EQUIPMENT**   None
**AIMS**   Lively physical activity; breathing control

Whole group sits in a large circle. One volunteer stands outside and on the word 'Go!' from Leader has to run round the circle counting each member of the group aloud '1, 2, 3, 4,' etc., without taking a breath, tapping each person lightly on the head on the way. When s/he runs out of breath, s/he can sit down and someone else can try to break the first volunteer's record.

## A27 SIMON SAYS

**EQUIPMENT**  None
**AIMS**  Physical control; alertness; co-ordination

Leader says 'Simon do this' and follows this by miming some action, e.g., scratching nose, or combing hair. Whole group has to follow this mime, but when Leader simply says 'Do this!', they should simply stand still. Obviously a speedy stream of instructions is essential in this game.

## A28 BRITISH BULLDOG

**EQUIPMENT**  None
**AIMS**  Group involvement; lively physical activity

This is another old but very popular game. All players except 1–3 volunteers stand at one end of the room. Volunteers stand in the centre. When Leader calls 'Over!' group standing at the end of the room has to run to the opposite end. If tagged by the volunteers, those running must freeze on the spot.

**A29**  **VARIATION**  Instead of running from end to end, try hopping on the left leg – or, even more sophisticated – hopping backwards.

**A30**  **VARIATION**  Get participants to *walk* across with their eyes closed, and limit those in the middle to one or two, who may or may not be allowed to keep their eyes open.

**A31**  **VARIATION**  Revert to the standard running procedure, but instruct those in the middle of the room trying to tag the others that they must work holding hands. Those running may only be tagged by the outer pair of hands one at each end of the linked group in the centre. When tagged in this way, the victim should link hands and join with his or her captors.

## A32 MOVE AROUND 1

**EQUIPMENT** Tape recorder
**AIMS** Lively physical activity; physical control; group co-operation

This is a simple but very effective activity if done properly. Select a lively piece of pop or rock music. (This is best played on a tape recorder with a pause button.) Tell the whole group to walk or move around any part of the room to the music, preferably responding to the beat of the music in the pace of movement adopted. Instruct everyone to listen carefully to the music. If individuals find themselves going in the same direction as anyone else, they should change direction quickly. When there is a pause and the music stops, however briefly, everyone must instantly turn as near to 360 degrees as possible (i.e. to the opposite direction) and continue moving as if nothing had happened. If performed *accurately* and swiftly, without bumping into anyone else, this is a difficult manoeuvre. Leader should ensure that some pauses come in fairly rapid succession, followed by some periods with no pauses. Remember to stress *accuracy* and *no bumping*. The larger the group, the more pauses, the smaller the space, the greater the control required.

**A33** **VARIATION** Reduce the space in which the group can operate.

**A34** **VARIATION** Slow down to the pace of a 'slow motion' film.

**A35** **VARIATION** Get members of the group to close their eyes when moving about.

19

## A36  MOVE AROUND 2

**EQUIPMENT**  Tape recorder, record player, tambourine or drum
**AIMS**  As in A32

Leader tells group to move around room to music as before. This time when Leader stops the music, group should change their mode of movement in use at that time. For example, if participants are walking at the pause, they then run or hop or jump. They cannot use the same way of getting about again. (If no music is available, Leader can beat a drum or shout 'Change'.)

## A37  VARIATION  Tell group that they must find different ways of moving without using their *feet* to move about the room.

## A38  GRAB A GROUP

**EQUIPMENT**  Tape recorder or record player
**AIMS**  Lively physical activity; arbitrary mixing of the group

This is a useful way of dividing the whole group into arbitrary sub-groups. Whole group to move about as before. This time when Leader stops the music s/he should shout out a number (e.g. '5!'). Participants then have to grab the people nearest to them to form a group of the correct number. (This is a good co-operation exercise!)

## A39  VARIATION  Get the whole group to form sub-groups with their eyes closed.

## A40  GROUP CALL-SIGN

**EQUIPMENT**  None
**AIMS**  Group involvement; to diminish self-consciousness; experimentation with sound

Leader divides group into sub-groups of five or six people (could combine with A38). Give these sub-groups a short period of time to create a call-sign by which they can recognise each other. Then bring whole group together in the centre of the room, and get everyone to close their eyes. Mix everyone up thoroughly, in silence, and then allow call-signs to begin. The object is for all members of each sub-group to find each other once more without cheating and opening their eyes.

## A41  SILLY WALKING

**EQUIPMENT**  Tape recorder or record player
**AIMS**  Lively physical activity; group participation/involvement; to diminish self-consciousness

Inspired by *Monty Python's Flying Circus*, this is a popular warm-up activity. Choose some bright, brisk music (a military march?) Get whole group to move around to this, but when Leader stops the music, each participant has to change to a silly, exaggerated walk. They must discover a completely different 'silly walk' after each pause.

## A42  WHERE'S YOUR MATE?

**EQUIPMENT**  Cards on which are written the names of pairs of animals, birds etc.
**PREPARATION**  For a group of 30, you will need to make 30 cards, with names of 15 pairs of different animals on them. For example, two cards will have 'Bee' written on them, two will have 'Hen', and so on. . . . Suggested animals might include: Bee, Hen, Lion, Sheep, Cow, Large Alsatian dog, small Poodle or Terrier dog, Rattlesnake, Gorilla, Parrot, Owl, Donkey, Pig, Elephant, Cuckoo, Cat.
**AIMS**  To diminish self-consciousness; group participation and involvement

21

Leader gives out the cards, making sure that the pairs of mates are well separated within the group and instructing the group to keep their animal identities secret. Then on the word 'Go!' individuals in the group should make the sound normally associated with their animal, all together. Pairs should then try to identify each other, without using human speech.

**A43** **VARIATION** Do *not* allow animal sounds. Partners should simply identify one another through *mime*.

## A44 MOVE TO THE BEAT

**EQUIPMENT**   A drum and beater, a table and a triangle
**AIMS**   Physical control and co-ordination

Leader beats a regular rhythm on the drum and gets group to move around room taking one pace for every beat. If Leader changes and begins to beat the table, group must respond immediately by walking backwards, again taking a pace every beat. If Leader begins beating time on the triangle, group must respond by stooping as low as they can, and walking forwards to the beat as best they can in that position. Leader should intersperse drum beats with table and triangle. This can be a physically exhausting and mind-battering exercise!

# B QUIETER CONCENTRATION EXERCISES

*These DRAMASTARTERS are all suggestions for quieter more concentrated activity which might be used after a period of lively physical exercise to begin to focus the group's attention and sharpen awareness. They can also be used at the end of the drama lesson to quieten the group or for relaxation.*

## B1 THE KEYS OF THE CASTLE

**EQUIPMENT**   A bunch of keys and a blindfold
**AIMS**   Concentration; ability to sit still; physical control and agility; ability to listen

Whole group sits in a large circle. One person volunteers to be blindfolded and sits in the centre of the circle, legs slightly apart. A bunch of keys should be placed on the ground in front of the blindfolded volunteer. Leader then silently chooses one of the group sitting in the circle to attempt to retrieve the keys without the volunteer in the centre hearing anything. The participant chosen should make a clockwise circuit *outside* the circle, only entering it when s/he has returned to the space where s/he had been sitting. Meanwhile, the blindfolded volunteer may, at any time, point in the direction where s/he thinks his or her challenger may be. If s/he scores a direct hit, another challenger can be chosen; if the challenger succeeds, *s/he* becomes the keeper of the keys.

## B2 SONAR SEARCH

**EQUIPMENT**   Two instruments, e.g. tambourines, shakers; two blindfolds
**AIMS**   Concentration; ability to sit still; ability to listen

Whole group sits in a large circle. Two volunteers stand in the centre and are blindfolded. They are each given one instrument which makes a sound, e.g. a tin filled with dried peas; tambourine or whistle. Each blindfolded volunteer is placed at some point inside the circle, and one is told s/he is the pursuer, the other that s/he is the pursued. The pursued is told that s/he must make a sound every ten seconds, and the pursuer that s/he must respond by making a sound of his or her own in reply to the first six rattles made by the pursued. After six rattles, the pursued must remain silent. The object is for pursuer to 'find' the pursued.

## B3   MAGIC MEMORY

**EQUIPMENT**   12–15 objects on a tray covered with a cloth; enough pencils and paper for each person
**PREPARATION**   Assemble objects – a matchbox, an apple etc. on tray
**AIMS**   Quiet concentration; recognition; memory recall

Who has the Magic Memory of the group? Whole group sits on floor in a circle, each with pencil and paper. Leader brings out cloth-covered tray. Group is allowed to see the contents of the tray for 30 seconds, and allowed a further 30 afterwards to write down as many objects as they can remember.

## B4   SOUND RECOGNITION

**EQUIPMENT**   Things which make a noise! See suggestions below
**PREPARATION**   Assemble about ten sound-producing objects
**AIMS**   Accurate listening; quiet concentration

Whole group sits in a line facing a wall, or simply with their eyes closed. Each participant should be ready with pencil and paper. Leader makes sounds in turn and group is then given time to write down what they thought they heard. Suggestions for easily-found sounds in classroom or studio: tearing paper, flicking through a book; turning on a light switch; using a stapling machine; sharpening a pencil; slapping a ruler on the leader's hand; drawing a curtain or adjusting a windowblind; opening a door; throwing a heavy book onto the floor; writing on a blackboard with chalk.

## B5  THE FEELIES

**EQUIPMENT**  Items which are interesting to feel! See suggestions below
**PREPARATION**  Suggestions for 'feelies' to assemble on tray – an uncooked sausage, a carrot, a tube of toothpaste, a calculator, a piece of 'Velcro', a pencil sharpener, an apple, a hard-boiled egg, some cotton wool, a screw, a shoe
**AIMS**  Quiet concentration; sensory perception; memory recall

Whole group sits in circle with eyes closed. Each participant has pencil and paper. Leader then passes ten or so objects for them to touch, hold, and then pass on to their neighbour. Time can be allowed afterwards to remember and write down any objects recognised.

## B6  SOMEONE'S MISSING

**EQUIPMENT**  None
**AIMS**  Group involvement; observation; quiet concentration; memory recall

Whole group sits on the floor, dotted around the room. One volunteer is asked to leave the room. After s/he has gone, Leader chooses someone else to leave (this must be by another route from the first). First volunteer can then return and try to spot who has gone.

**B7**  **VARIATION**  Make the whole exercise more difficult by rearranging the positions of the group while Volunteer 1 is out of the room.

## B8 FREEZE IN ROLE

**EQUIPMENT** None

**AIMS** Concentration; quiet involvement; beginnings of mime

Leader tells whole group to walk quietly and calmly around the room, making sure that no-one else walks in the same direction. On the words 'Freeze as a . . .', followed by an occupation, from the Leader, each person must quickly adopt the characteristic pose of the occupation which the leader has just named, and then *freeze*. Leader should then walk around to see how effective these frozen effigies are. Some suggestions of occupations: hairdresser, teacher, farmer, pop singer, bus conductor, film star.

**B9** **VARIATION** Try more difficult, less 'tangible' subjects. For example, Anger, Envy, Sorrow, Death, Birth, Despair, Boredom, Domination, Acquiescence, Mirth.

## B10 LOOK AROUND YOU

**EQUIPMENT** None

**AIMS** Quiet concentration and involvement; getting to know a space; sensory perception.

Leader tells whole group to spread out in the room, find a space and sit down. Leader then asks everyone to look around the room very carefully, making a very detailed observation of everything. After a short time, Leader tells group that s/he is going to give them a letter of the alphabet, and, after hearing it everyone must run and touch three objects in the room which begin with that letter. For example, 'D!' (door, dust, desk?) As soon as they have touched three objects beginning with the correct letter, participants should sit down. After each letter, Leader should find out what has been touched and should encourage thoughtful or unusual items to be spotted and touched.

**B11**   VARIATION   Ask for three textures (soft, coarse, smooth etc.) or three colours.

## B12   PROGRAMMED RESPONSE

**EQUIPMENT**   None
**AIMS**   Quiet concentration; physical control

Leader instructs whole group to find a space and sit down on the floor somewhere in the room. Participants should then make themselves as small as possible by curling up in a ball. After a short time, Leader instructs the group to get up from their smallest to their tallest position, standing with their arms reaching as high as they can, stretching hard on the tips of their toes. Group is now told that in a few seconds they are to revert to their former smallest position on the floor, but that they must programme their movements to coincide with Leader completing a number count from 1 to 20, so that by the time Leader reaches 20, they will be in their smallest position. Group should be warned to keep their movements as smooth as possible, and not jerk each time the Leader calls out another number.

**B13**   VARIATION   Leader counts at a faster or slower rate. Sometimes the group work better with their eyes closed.

## B14   TAKE A DEEP BREATH

**EQUIPMENT**   None
**AIMS**   Concentration; absorption; breathing control.

Leader tells whole group to find their own space and lie down on the floor on their backs, as comfortably as possible, closing their eyes. Leader then tells everyone to inhale deeply on the word 'Now!' and only to stop taking in breath when s/he says 'Stop!' Group holds that breath until Leader says 'Release!'

## B15 FIND YOUR WAY BACK

**EQUIPMENT**   Blindfolds (optional for B15)
**AIMS**   Concentration; sensory exploration

This is a good follow-on from B14. Participants should be sitting in a space of their own on the floor. Leader tells them to examine that space very carefully, and to feel the texture of the floor at that point. Then Leader poses the thought: 'If there were no light in this room, and you couldn't see, would there be a way of finding your exact position once more, if you were to travel from some other and at present unknown point in the room?' Group is then allowed to speculate, and is given two minutes to work out for themselves a system for finding their way back. When the time is up, each participant is invited to take a last look at his or her position, then to stand with eyes closed (or be blindfolded). Leader then gives the group instructions which should take participants, still with eyes closed, well away from their original positions (e.g. take three paces forward, turn to the right, take another two paces, turn to the left, take five paces, and so on). The aim is to disorientate them, before they have to find their way back. Group is then told to attempt to return to their original positions without opening their eyes. Give them an allotted length of time, before telling everyone to 'freeze', then they can open their eyes and see how near they have managed to get.

**B16**   **VARIATION**   Provide everyone with a blindfold; many fewer will find their way back accurately!

## B17 MEATY MOVEMENT

**EQUIPMENT**   None
**AIMS**   Physical control; the beginnings of creative movement

Leader tells participants to find their own space on the floor, and curl up into their smallest position. They are then invited to imagine that the drama studio, or room in which they are working, has become one vast supermarket refrigerated display cabinet, and that they have become joints of meat, encased in cling-film. Leader invites speculation on what it might feel like to be enclosed so tightly in such a material. Group is then instructed to begin to try to stretch the cling-film which is covering them, so that eventually they can, after quite a struggle, stand up, and break out of this plastic prison.

## B18  MOVE A JOINT

**EQUIPMENT**  None
**AIMS**  Quiet but rigorous physical exercise; co-ordination

(This follows-on well from B17!) Members of the group should stand in their own space with both hands in front of them. They should begin by moving both of their little fingers backwards and forwards ten times. The aim is to add another joint after every tenth movement. Leader could suggest the following sequence: Little finger, followed by each of the other fingers, followed by thumb, then all fingers together, then hands, elbows, shoulders, neck and head, waist, and whole body in as many places as possible. Once a joint has started to move it should not stop (i.e. little fingers should still be moving until the end).

## B19  LIE AND LISTEN

**EQUIPMENT**  Pencil and paper (optional)
**AIMS**  Relaxation; quietner; listening concentration

This could be used after lively physical activity (B18?). Leader tells participants to find their own space and lie down as comfortably as possible on their backs; then to close their eyes and listen to the sounds around. How many can they hear? How *far* can they hear? What sounds can be heard *inside* the room, and what sounds *outside?* Get them to make a mental note of each, and then, after an allotted length of time, to sit up and share what they have heard with the rest of the group, or to write as many down as they can remember.

## B20  FOLLOW THAT VOICE

**EQUIPMENT**  None
**AIMS**  Quiet concentration; group co-operation; relaxation; listening; beginning to speak

Leader tells participants to lie in their own space with their eyes closed as in B19. When all are in position, Leader chooses one participant who must start telling a story. Rest of group can then be invited by Leader to begin crawling towards where they think the voice is, keeping their eyes closed. They should be reminded to proceed with caution as other people may be in their way.

## B21  WHO'S SPEAKING?

**EQUIPMENT**  None
**AIMS**  As in B20

Group should be in position as in B19/B20. When everyone is lying down with eyes closed, Leader tells group that s/he is going to choose some people to do some talking. If individuals feel a tap on their head, they must begin speaking. They can say anything they like (within limits!) but they must continue talking clearly and fairly loudly until they feel a second tap, at which point they must cease. Rest of group is asked to identify who was speaking.

*The following DRAMASTARTERS are all simple ideas for movement exercises. To provide a suitable atmosphere for concentration and involvement, I try to ensure that such activities are performed in silence.*

## B22  WALKABOUT 1

**EQUIPMENT**  None
**AIMS**  Concentration; beginnings of creative movement; whole group participation

Group should walk about room as naturally as possible. Leader then tells participants to walk as far away from everyone else as possible. S/he then instructs them to walk as near to everyone else as possible.

**B23**  VARIATION  Get group to close their eyes.

**B24**  VARIATION  Instruct group to walk as slowly or as quickly as possible without running.

## B25  WALKABOUT 2

**EQUIPMENT**  None
**AIMS**  Diminish self-consciousness; group involvement; creative movement

Some ideas to try for movement: Leader invites group to walk about the room as someone who is 85; someone who is nervous; someone who is angry; someone who is forgetful; someone who is shy; someone who is cold or someone who is weak. It is even better if Leader 'talks through' a fictional situation for each mode of movement.

## B26  WEATHER CONDITIONS WALKABOUT

**EQUIPMENT**  None
**AIMS**  Concentration; creative movement

Leader suggests a variety of weather/atmospheric conditions for the group to imagine they are walking around in. Suggestions might include: thick fog; high wind; driving rain; walking on ice; through deep snow; in heavy, thick mud; wading through waist-high water; splashing in puddles; walking in desert-hot sunshine.

## B27 MOVE OVER THERE

**EQUIPMENT** None
**AIMS** Physical control; concentration; group co-operation

Leader tells participants to find their own space anywhere in the room. They are then told to fix a point at the other side of the room on the floor and to stare at it intently. On the word 'Move!' from the Leader, they are to move to that point carefully and evenly, pacing themselves so that they do not need to stop or alter course to allow someone else to pass in front of them, or to touch anyone else while they are making their journey.

## B28 ESTIMATE A MINUTE

**EQUIPMENT** None
**AIMS** Relaxation; quiet concentration

Leader tells participants to find their own space, and sit down on the floor with their eyes closed. Leader instructs them to put up their hands when they think one minute has passed, and then carefully times one minute, announcing when the correct time has elapsed. Who was closest?

*So far these movement/concentration/relaxation exercises have largely been solo pursuits. The following suggestions are for pairs, moving on to larger group work.*

## B29 BACK-TO-BACK

**EQUIPMENT** None
**AIMS** Pair trust; physical contact

Leader divides whole group into pairs. Partners stand back-to-back, with arms linked at the elbows. Leader then instructs them to sit down, without breaking the arm-link, and then to stand up again.

## B30 KEEP A STRAIGHT FACE

**EQUIPMENT** None
**AIMS** Quiet concentration; absorption; pair involvement

Leader divides whole group into pairs. They are instructed to stand, facing one another, 60cm (2') apart. They should then be instructed to look down at their own feet and adopt a serious face. (This is often difficult in itself!) On the word 'Go!' from Leader, they look up into each other's eyes, maintaining the serious expression of their faces for as long as they are able. Both members of the pair must sit down when either one breaks concentration.

**B31** **VARIATION** Try out the same exercise in sub-groups of three, four or more!

## B32 TRUST YOUR PARTNER

**EQUIPMENT** None
**AIMS** Concentration; pair trust

(Whole group works in pairs again.) Leader instructs one partner to stand behind the other. Partner in front is then told to lean backwards and is supported by his or her partner behind. Reverse roles.

## B33 CHAIR TRUST

**EQUIPMENT** One chair per pair
**AIMS** Concentration; control; trust.

(Whole group works in pairs again.) Leader instructs each pair to provide themselves with one chair, decide who is A and who is B, find a space away from other pairs. A sits on the chair and B blindfolds A. B then stands behind the chair. Leader then asks the blindfolded As to stand up, and tells Bs to remove the chair, carrying it some distance away from A before returning and silently replacing it in a position which, while not actually touching the back of A's legs, would ensure that A could sit down with confidence, knowing that s/he could trust B to have placed the chair correctly. When Leader is satisfied that all chairs have been correctly positioned, s/he can instruct all As to sit down, without feeling behind them with their hands. Then A and B should reverse roles.

**B34**  VARIATION   Leader *could* introduce an element of doubt that the chair is really there, before getting the blindfolded member of the pair to sit. Some people believe that the extra relief felt afterwards heightens the feeling of mutual trust between the pair!

## B35  WALKABOUT TRUST

EQUIPMENT   Blindfolds – one per pair
AIMS   Pair trust; sensory perception

(Whole group works in pairs, with one partner blindfolded.) Sighted partner A should lead the blindfolded B on a journey around the drama studio or classroom. A should take B to four objects in the room, which B should be allowed to touch and identify. Then the two should reverse roles.

## B36  ROBOT CONTROL

EQUIPMENT   None or blindfolds – one per pair
AIMS   Pair trust; group co-operation

*'Best lesson I've had in ages. Now for the freeze button.'*

(Whole group works in pairs again, with one partner
blindfolded.) Leader instructs pairs to allocate each partner a
letter – A or B. A becomes the robot, and must work at all
times, controlled by B. A should be blindfolded, or work with
eyes closed. B should control A in the following way: s/he
should tap A *once* between the shoulder-blades (gently!) if s/he
wishes A to begin moving forwards, and *twice* in the same place
if s/he wants A to stop. To get A to turn right, B should simply
tap A on the *right* shoulder; likewise a tap on the left shoulder
instructs A to turn left. Leader should stress *no talking* between
partners. After a while B should become the robot and A the
controller.

**B37** VARIATION *Reverse* control commands. Controller taps robot's left shoulder if s/he wishes him or her to turn *right*, and s/he taps right shoulder if he or she wishes robot to turn *left*.

**B38** VARIATION Leader informs group that s/he has a master control over all robots' speed. Leader can then vary speed of movement from slow-motion to high-velocity!

**B39** VARIATION Construct an obstacle course of chairs/tables around which controllers must steer their robots.

## B40 FLOOR CONTACT

EQUIPMENT None
AIMS Co-operation; involvement; physical contact

(Whole group works in pairs again.) Leader explains that each pair has a total of eight possible 'points of contact' with the floor. For the purposes of this exercise, these are each participant's two hands and feet. When the leader calls out a number (between 1 and 8), each pair must link themselves physically in some way and present that number of 'points of contact' touching the floor. For example, if Leader calls out '3!', each pair must be linked together and must have three feet (or a combination of hands and feet) touching the floor. Encourage unusual or outrageous postures, and finish with the smallest *floor contact* of 1!

**B41** VARIATION Allow larger groups of three or more (extending the maximum number of points of contact accordingly).

## B42 TRIO TRUST

EQUIPMENT None
AIMS Larger trust exercise; creative movement

Leader divides whole group into threes. Each person in the three is given a letter – **A**, **B** or **C**. **A** must stand facing **C**, about 60–90cm (2–3′) away. **B** must stand between them facing **C**, and imagine that his or her feet are hinged to the floor. This makes **B** fixed to the floor, but able to rock backwards and forwards. Leader then instructs **B** to make his or her whole body rigid, and then lean backwards to be supported by **A**. When **B** is fully supported by **A**, **A** must then guide **B** back to the upright position and on towards **C**. As soon as **B** is upright, **C** must begin to take over from **A** and take **B**'s weight. **C** then returns **B** to the upright position, and then directs **B** backwards to **A** again. Leader should periodically stop trios, and get more successful threes to show the rest. **A** and **C** should take a turn in the centre too.

## B43   REMOTE CONTROL

**EQUIPMENT**   One blindfold for each trio
**AIMS**   Trust; listening; group co-operation

(Again, whole group works in sub-groups of three.) Each member of the trio is given a letter – **A**, **B** or **C**. Leader explains that **C** will shortly be blindfolded. Can the trio work out for themselves a method of communication which does *not* involve using *words*, by which **C** could be guided to walk from **A** standing at one end of the room to **B** standing at the other? Give the groups a couple of minutes or so to work out their system of communication. Then stand **A**s and **C**s at one end of the room, with **C** blindfolded. Leader then positions **B**s at the other end of the room, making certain that they are *not* standing directly opposite the other members of their trio. Leader then invites the remote controlling to begin. After the first attempt, groups can see for themselves the difficulties of communicating at the same time as other groups, and may wish to devise other means of communication as a result when **A** and **B** have their turn at being blindfolded.

**B44**  VARIATION   Place an obstacle course of chairs in the middle of the room *after* those who are to cross from one side to the other have been blindfolded.

## B45  BODY TALK

**EQUIPMENT**   None
**AIMS**   Larger group co-operation; physical control; physical contact

This activity builds on the group co-operation established so far by working in groups of at least six to a maximum of 10 or 12. Leader explains that the groups must imagine that they are trying to communicate with an airplane flying directly above them, but can only use their bodies to do so. On instructions from Leader, they must use their bodies to create the letters s/he gives them. They must use *every* member of the group each time, and must remain lying on the floor in position until their 'letter' shape has been identified by the Leader. Suggested letters: S – O – S to begin with, followed by any letter of the alphabet.

**B46**  VARIATION   Give each sub-group a different letter which together spell a word or message.

**B47**  VARIATION   Include punctuation: , . ; " ! ?

**B48**  VARIATION   Ask groups to form shapes: square, circle, triangle, oblong, cube, etc.

**B49**  VARIATION   Get groups to create buildings or objects with their bodies. *Suggestions*: a large cathedral, a block of flats, an ornate fountain, a rocket-launch pad.

**B50**  VARIATION Groups not allowed to communicate with words or sounds during any of the preceding activities B45–8.

*The following suggestions for mime exercises also move from solo activity to pair to larger group work.*

## B51   SOLO MIME

**EQUIPMENT**   None
**AIMS**   Quiet concentration; beginnings of mime

Leader tells whole group to spread out and for individuals to
find their own space and sit down. Leader should stress that for
Solo Mime to succeed it is vital to ignore everyone else, and to
work silently and independently. *Activity suggestions*: washing
hands and then face, then drying both. (Then try cold water?)
Touch something hot; shave or put on make-up at a mirror; put
sugar into, then drink, a cup of tea; take a spoonful of medicine
you know is going to taste awful; eat a cream cake which is
overflowing with cream. Stress accurate, controlled movement.

## B52   SOLO MIME SEQUENCE

**EQUIPMENT**   None
**AIMS**   Concentration; mime skills; absorption

(Participants work on their own as in B51.) This time Leader
'talks group through' a mime sequence. Everyone is told to lie
down and imagine that they are lying in some long grass beside
a lake. They can feel the sun beating down on them, and the
sound of a distant skylark. Suddenly, a small insect, a flying ant,
lands on their face . . . (pause) eventually it disappears.
Gradually they begin to feel thirsty . . . they sit up . . . and
reach for a bottle of lemonade next to them . . . the top is
difficult to unscrew at first . . . but then they get it off . . . and
take a good long drink . . . which makes them hiccup. . . . Then
they decide to have a sandwich as they are beginning to feel
particularly hungry . . . they search around for the packet of
sandwiches made for them that morning . . . find it . . . gently
open it . . . take out a sandwich . . . examine it . . . and then
take a huge bite which is almost too much to cram into their
mouth . . . then they discover that the sandwich was filled with

something which tastes like dried cat food! . . . They decide to feed the rest of the sandwiches to the ducks swimming on the lake in front of them. . . .

## B53 MOOD MIME

**EQUIPMENT** None
**AIMS** Slightly more advanced mime work; quiet concentration

(Again, participants work on their own.) Leader invites participants to choose their own mime on anything they might do around the house, e.g., washing up. Leader allows a short amount of time for this mime, then stops the group. Leader then invites the group to continue with the mime they have chosen, but this time giving the impression that they are *angry* about something. *Other moods*: anxious, nervous, bored, unhappy, harassed; forgetful.

## B54 MIRROR MIME

**EQUIPMENT** None
**AIMS** Mime in pairs; pair co-operation and involvement

(Whole group works in pairs, each partner with the letter **A** or **B**.) Leader explains that **A** is standing in front of a mirror, represented by **B**. (**A** and **B** should stand facing one another about 60–90cm (2–3′) apart.) **B** must attempt to mirror exactly any movement **A** might make. After a short time, **A** becomes the mirror and **B** the person standing in front of it.

## B55 PAIR MIME

**EQUIPMENT** None
**AIMS** As B54

(Whole group works in pairs.) *Suggestions for activity*: bowling and batting in a game of cricket; playing tennis; table-tennis; a game of chess; putting up some shelves; erecting a tent.

## B56   GROUP MIME

**EQUIPMENT**   None
**AIMS**   Group co-operation and involvement; more advanced mime skills

(Whole group works in sub-groups of four to six.) Leader invites these sub-groups to spend some time working out their own mime sequence. This might be a family meal time, or a team game, or workers on a factory conveyer belt, or something of their own choice. Each sequence must have a definite beginning, middle and end.

**B57**   **VARIATION**   Perform the sequence in slow-motion or at top speed like an old silent movie.

## B58   PASS THE MIME

**EQUIPMENT**   None
**AIMS**   Whole group involvement; diminishing self-consciousness; refining mime skills

Whole group stands in a circle, facing outwards. Leader takes one participant out of the circle and mimes some action (e.g. sewing on a shirt button) to him or her secretly. This person then returns to his or her place in the circle and reproduces this mime as accurately as possible to the neighbour on his or her right, who then does likewise. Everyone must make sure they are looking away, until it is their turn to receive the mime. Like the game *Chinese Whispers*, the difference between the mime at the start and at the finish is often staggering!

## B59  WHO'S DOING IT?

**EQUIPMENT**  None
**AIMS**  Refining mime skills; group co-operation and involvement

Whole group sits in a large circle on the floor. Leader chooses one volunteer to leave the room. While s/he is away, Leader chooses one of the group to lead the mime. When the first volunteer comes back into the room, the mime leader must begin to mime any action of his or her choice, and the rest of the group must immediately begin to copy mime leader. S/he can change the mime action at any time, and the rest of the group must follow. The volunteer who left the room must guess who is leading the group in their miming.

## B60  PASS THE PINCH

**EQUIPMENT**  None
**AIMS**  Group co-operation and involvement; relaxation; quiet concentration

Whole group sits in a large circle on the floor, Leader as well, holding hands. (This often calls for a great deal of group trust in itself!) Everyone *except* Leader must close their eyes. When this is accomplished, Leader squeezes briefly his or her left-hand neighbour's hand three times. Group is told that they must pass this 'message' on to their neighbour, and it eventually should return to the Leader's right hand, in, we hope, the same form. Leader should time how long this takes, and the group should work towards speed and accuracy of transmission.

# C SPEECH ACTIVITIES

*The basic aim behind all the suggestions for games and activities in this section is to move the lesson onwards towards improvisation, and, by implication, oral work. These DRAMASTARTERS are devised to try to make that process as painless and as easy as possible, and to involve even the shyest and orally most reluctant members of the group in speech work which will prepare them for more demanding improvisations in the final stages of the Drama lesson. In English they can be used as excellent preparatory exercises for oral work.*

## C1 COUNT ME IN

**EQUIPMENT** None
**AIMS** First moves towards oral work; pair involvement

Leader divides whole group into pairs and instructs pairs to allocate each partner a letter – **A** or **B**. When Leader says 'Go', **A** has to begin counting aloud regularly and rhythmically up to 40 in two's (2, 4, 6, etc.) and **B** in three's up to 39. **A** and **B** must count *both at the same time*. Repeat the exercise with each trying to make the other *fail* to count successfully.

## C2 SIMULTANEOUS SPEECH

**EQUIPMENT** None
**AIMS** Speech work; pair to larger group involvement

(Whole group works in pairs again, each partner with the letter **A** or **B**.) Leader gives everyone some time to think about the following: As have to remember everything which has happened to them today so far from waking up, and be prepared to relate this to Bs. B must remember a day's outing somewhere recently and must get ready to tell **A**. Naturally they are both going to speak at once, on the Leader's command 'Go!' How much did each partner hear from the other?

**C3** **VARIATION** Try the same exercise in threes: **A**, **B**, **C**. **A** and **B** have to tell **C** their own versions of the subjects mentioned in C2, and, in some way other than physical force, **A** and **B** must try to ensure that it is *their* story that **C** hears. Afterwards, discuss what **C** heard and why. *Alternative topics*: a detailed description of a person the speaker knows well; recounting a recent argument or disagreement in detail.

## C4 FOLLOW-ON

**EQUIPMENT** None
**AIMS** Speech work; pair to larger group involvement

(Whole group works in pairs, each with the letter **A** or **B**.) **A** begins the first word of a sentence, **B** must follow-on with the next word of the sentence, which should obviously fit in with the first. **A** then contributes the next word of the sentence, and so on.

**C5** **VARIATION** Increase the size of the group, possibly even up to the whole group.

## C6 SHOPPING LIST

**EQUIPMENT** None
**AIMS** Speaking in front of whole group; memory recall

Whole group sits in a large circle Leader chooses one person to begin. S/he has to say 'Yesterday I went shopping and I bought . . .' putting in what s/he bought at the end. Participant on his or her right then has to repeat the same formula 'Yesterday I went shopping and I bought . . .' S/he then has to remember the first person's purchase and add one of his or her own. The person on his or her right then has to recall the first two purchases, using the same formula, and again, add one of his or her own. This continues round the circle, until every member has contributed to the shopping-list. Leader might encourage extravagant purchases!

## C7 NAME RECALL

**EQUIPMENT** None
**AIMS** 'Getting-to-know-you' introductory exercise; speaking in front of whole group; memory recall; listening

Whole group sits in a large circle. Leader chooses one person to begin, who says, 'My name is . . .' adding his or her first name. Participant on his or her right has to say. 'His/her name is . . .', pointing to left-hand neighbour, and giving neighbour's first name, then adding 'My name is . . .', adding his or her own. This continues right around the circle.

## C8 ANSWER THAT 'PHONE

**EQUIPMENT** Real or imaginary telephone
**AIMS** Speaking in front of whole group; listening; memory recall

Whole group sits in a large circle. For the best effect a real telephone should be placed in the centre. Each member of the group should be numbered consecutively. When the Leader calls out a number at random, the participant holding it should leave his or her place and answer the telephone convincingly. S/he should then have a conversation with an imaginary caller and cannot stop talking until the Leader calls another number. The person on the telephone at that point must replace the receiver and return to his or her place, and the next member of the group must come out and answer the 'phone. An imaginary or toy telephone must suffice if a real one is not available.

## C9 VARIATION

Get subsequent members of the group to *continue* the first volunteer's 'phone call and *not* start new ones each time.

## C10   COMMUNAL STORYTELLING

**EQUIPMENT**   None
**AIMS**   Speaking in front of whole group; listening; memory recall

Whole group sits in a circle, individuals numbered consecutively. Leader chooses a number and the participant holding it must begin the story with the words 'There once was . . .', adding the opening few sentences. S/he must continue talking until Leader calls out the next number, who must continue the story maintaining consistency of plot, characters etc.

*'I asked for **facts**, Dumpton, not sensational revelations.'*

## C11    MOVE ON

**EQUIPMENT**    None
**AIMS**    Talking; listening; memory recall; speaking, at the end of the exercise, to whole group; getting-to-know-you exercise

(Whole group works in pairs, each with the letter **A** or **B**.) Leader tells all **A**s to tell their partner three facts about themselves, and when **A** has finished for **B** to tell **A** three facts about him or herself. All **A**s then move on to a new **B** and tell him or her three *new* facts. The process is repeated until each **A** has visited five **B**s. The whole group then assembles together in a circle, whereupon Leader tries to build up a picture of each member, based on information supplied by those s/he has spoken to.

## C12    LIFE STORY

**EQUIPMENT**    None
**AIMS**    Talking; listening; pair involvement; memory recall; good 'getting to know you' introductory exercise

(Whole group works in pairs, each with the letter **A** or **B**.) Leader tells participants to think of ten important events in their own life from birth to the present day. After time to think, **A** must relate these to **B**, followed by **B** telling **A**. Whole group then gets together, sitting in a circle, and each person must introduce their partner using the formula: 'This is . . .' (first name), followed by the ten details about his or her life so far.

## C13    HOT POTATO

**EQUIPMENT**    A small object to be passed round
**AIMS**    Speaking; listening; memory recall

Whole group sits in a circle. Leader presents the group with a small object (not necessarily a potato!) which will be passed around. S/he explains that as soon as it is put into the hands of a person sitting in the circle, that person will have to begin talking, and cannot stop talking until their neighbour reaches for the object. The participant who is holding the object at any one time cannot decide when s/he is going to pass on the 'hot potato', but must wait until the neighbour on his or her left-hand side takes the object, before s/he can stop talking. The neighbour must begin speaking as soon as the object touches his or her hands.

**C14**　VARIATION　Get first person to receive the object to begin a story, and the rest of the group to continue it.

## C15　OBJECT LESSON

EQUIPMENT　Cards (see below)
PREPARATION　Assemble a set of cards, each with the name of an everyday object written on it. *Suggestions*: drawing pin, house brick, hairdryer, frying pan, long-playing record.
AIMS　Speaking in front of the group; listening; whole-group involvement

Leader selects a number and the participant holding it must stand in the centre of the circle. S/he must then attempt to describe what the object *looks* like. S/he can say what the object is made of, but must not actually *name* it, or say what it is used for. S/he should simply describe the object's physical appearance, size etc. Members of the group should attempt to name the object. When they are successful, Leader should choose another participant to present the 'Object Lesson'.

**C16**　VARIATION　Use cards on which are written the names of famous personalities, and get participants to describe their physical appearance, *not* the actual name of their occupation. *Suggestions*: The Queen, Adolf Hitler, Winston Churchill, Mohammed Ali, Margaret Thatcher, Laurel and Hardy, Mickey Mouse.

# C17 CHOOSE YOUR IDENTITY

**EQUIPMENT** None

**AIMS** Beginnings of character or identity building; first steps at verbalising about this; listening

Leader divides whole group into sub-groups of eight to ten. Participants should sit in their groups in a tight circle on the floor. Leader invites each participant to create a new identity for him or her self selecting information from the alternatives s/he is about to give them. (At this stage group should be asked to restrict themselves to only the information supplied by Leader.) Leader tells group that they must choose a first name from: Betty, Juliet, Mary, or Christina, if they are a girl; from Alfred, Dave, Donald, Nicholas, Steve, if they are a boy. Then they should select a surname from: Martin, Cooper, Williamson, McPherson, Young, or Langdon-Davies. Leader then gives a number of options, each with four or so choices which participants within each group may choose for their own character. *Suggestions*: *Age*: 19, 23, 35, 52; *Lives in*: Southampton, Edinburgh, Bradford, Northampton; *Occupation*: hairdresser, bank clerk; typist, salesman/woman; *Family situation*: married/single/divorced; Children: 1, 2, 3, none; etc. Leader should ask participants to memorise their character's details. Sub-groups can then listen to each other trying to recall as many of the options as they can. Each person should begin 'My character was called . . .' and go on from there. The number of possible character permutations is surprising, and intriguing.

**C18** **VARIATION** Get participants to imagine that *they* are the characters they have just invented, and to move on to work with someone from another sub-group, introducing themselves in role and finding out about each other.

**C19** **VARIATION** Form new sub-groups of 10–12. Groups are to imagine that they have assumed the identity of the person they have created. The group is now at a party. All are strangers who should try to get to know each other. Individuals could add new information if Leader wants this.

## C20  OBJECTS FROM OUTER SPACE

**EQUIPMENT**   One everday object for each member of the group; watch or stop-watch for C21
**AIMS**   Structured talking; listening; pair to larger group involvement

Leader gives each member of the group an everyday object, e.g. stapler, light-bulb, comb, bottle-opener, clothes hanger, etc. Each participant is asked to imagine that he or she had found this object on a distant planet, retrieved it, and brought it back to earth. They are asked to make up such details as: What is it made out of? What was it used for? How did it work? Where and how was it found? What was it called? Participants are invited to create these imaginary details for themselves, which must not in any way resemble the object's current usage or composition. Leader gives everyone time to think, possibly allowing notes to be made. Then group is divided into pairs, each partner telling each other as much as they can about their object from outer space.

**C21**   **VARIATION**   Get into groups of five or six. Leader then tells everyone that they must give a one-minute talk on their object to the others in these small sub-groups. (Leader can time this.) If anyone 'dries' before a minute has elapsed, rest of sub-group must help out by asking questions about the object. Sub-groups should select the most effective speaker to compete against the best from other sub-groups and whole group could vote for the overall winner.

**C22**   **VARIATION**   Use pieces of driftwood, or ornate stones or pebbles.

50

## C23 LOCAL RADIO STREET INTERVIEWS

**EQUIPMENT**   Portable tape-recorder
**AIMS**   Beginnings of whole group improvisation; talking, relevant to a given situation

(It is best if each group can use a portable tape-recorder for this exercise.) Leader divides whole group into two large groups of 10–15. Each group must elect an interviewer who can record street interviews. Both can form queues two to three deep. *Suggested queues and interview topics*: *Queue* for a football match (much lively banter here!) *Subject*: Football hooliganism. *Queue* at supermarket checkout – *Subject*: Rising prices. *Queue* at Job Centre or DHSS – *Subject*: Unemployment – problems and frustrations. *Queue* for school canteen – *Subject*: School dinners, school uniform or school rules. Queues could be encouraged to make suitable background noises while interviews are being conducted.

*The following DRAMASTARTERS are all simple improvisations. I find it best to begin this important part of oral/drama work in small units and to work gradually towards larger group situations once students have developed some self-confidence. The suggestions here are therefore designed for use in pairs.*

## C24 I WAS FIRST HERE

**EQUIPMENT**   Bench or two chairs
**AIMS**   Beginnings of pair improvisation; talking; listening; intonation

(Whole group works in pairs, each with the letter **A** or **B**.) Leader tells all **A**s that they are office workers who for many years have visited the same park-bench to eat their lunch. Today they have arrived to sit on the accustomed seat when they discover an old tramp (played by **B**s) is lying there. What happens?

**C25**    **VARIATION**    After trying out the improvisation as suggested in C24, Leader invites pairs to try it out again, this time *not* using words but talking in letters of the alphabet. So that instead of **A** saying 'Excuse me I usually sit here,' and **B** replying 'Tough luck, mate.' **A** would say 'ABCDEFG' and **B** would reply 'XY, LLD!' The object is for meaning to be conveyed through the intonation used.

**C26**    **VARIATION**    Allow pairs to make up their own gobbledegook!

## C27   CUSTOMER COMPLAINT

**EQUIPMENT**    Table for counter
**AIMS**    Simple pair improvisation; talking; listening

(Whole group works in pairs, each with the letter A or B.) Leader tells pairs to set up a rudimentary 'shop'. Leader speaks to all As separately, telling them that they are going to be customers taking an article back to change in a shop. They can decide what that item is, and whether they are reasonable or unreasonable customers. While As are thinking about this, Leader addresses all Bs, telling them that they are shopkeepers, but that they won't know what kind of shop they work in until their customer brings back their purchase. However, Bs are given complete freedom to decide how they are going to react to the complaint, whether they are eager, concerned shopkeepers, or unfair or uninterested. Leader should stress that pairs must *co-operate* in story-building. For example, if A decides to 'bring in' a hamster, B must accept the idea that this is a pet shop.

## C28   DOOR-TO-DOOR SALESMAN

**EQUIPMENT**    Two chairs per pair
**AIMS**    Pair improvisation; talking; listening

(Whole group works in pairs each with the letter A or B, as in C27.) Leader instructs all As and all Bs separately again. Bs should equip themselves with two chairs, and imagine they are sitting in their living room at home. They should be told that they are suspicious of strangers calling at their homes, and can expect a visit from one shortly. As should be told that they are door-to-door salespeople, who are trying to sell a certain product, which they may choose. Unfortunately, they haven't actually got that product with them. (They must make up a convincing reason why.) Can they interest a customer in their product, and extract a deposit for it, without actually having to show the customer the product? Leader should encourage pairs to go through a mime sequence of a salesman or woman ringing a doorbell, householder answering etc. Afterwards find out what was being sold, and who had success.

**C29**  VARIATION   Leader instructs the householders, unknown to the salespeople, that they are hard of hearing.

## C30   POLICE INTERROGATION

EQUIPMENT   Two chairs per pair
AIMS   Pair improvisation; talking; listening

(Whole group works in pairs, each with a letter **A** or **B**. Leader issues instructions to all As and all Bs separately, as in C27.) Leader tells all As that they are to equip themselves with two chairs which should face each other. They are told to sit on one and wait. Leader tells As that they are sitting in a police interview room, and have been waiting there for nearly an hour. They will not learn their suspected 'crime' until the interview begins. Bs are told that they are Police Inspectors. Leader gives them a short time to make up some fictional details of what crime Suspect **A** has allegedly committed, and various details associated with it, such as when and where the crime was committed, how **A** was arrested etc. **A** must try to argue his or her way out of this difficult situation. Leader must again stress pair co-operation in building up the storyline.

# D LARGER IMPROVISATIONS

Writing about Drama, the Bullock Report *A Language for Life* (DES, 1975) noted 'drama has an obvious and substantial contribution to the development of children's language and its possibilities in this respect have yet to be fully explored' (p. 156). It added that 'in most schools drama has yet to realise its potential in helping the child to communicate with others, to express his own feelings and thoughts and to gain confidence in a variety of contexts.' (p. 161)

One of the most successful ways of achieving these worthy aims is through the use of improvisation, and the games and exercises in *Dramastarters*, when used progressively and as part of a structured lesson plan (for lesson suggestions see section E), are all designed to lead towards improvisation as a main focus and activity.

Clearly, if drama is to make a useful contribution to 'the development of children's language', improvisations must present pupils with situations which are comprehensive, varied, and, above all, relevant. If it is to enable students 'to gain confidence in a variety of contexts' it must be a progressive and gradual process.

So far, the oral language activity suggested in *Dramastarters*, has demanded of each individual student only short, controlled periods of solo verbalisation in front of the whole group, and more extended, though essentially private, periods in simple pair improvisations. This section offers some basic ideas for larger group situations. *Dramastarters*, however, is meant to be a collection of suggestions which are, essentially, *ways in* to drama. It does not fall within the scope of this book to offer more *detailed* stimulus material for improvisations.

Despite their brevity, *Dramastarters* in this section still lend themselves to sustained, more advanced drama work, and could easily form the main activity of drama lessons. Group leaders can investigate how best to use these ideas, but they are designed for groups of four upwards, and should lend themselves best to a time allowance of at least twenty to thirty minutes, within the lesson. Sometimes the resulting improvisations should be spontaneous and essentially private, occasionally they could be polished and shown to the rest of the group.

*One way in to improvisations is to give groups cards on which are written a few words which might be spoken in the course of the scene. Alternatively, Leader can suggest that the words on the card might simply reflect the subject matter of the improvisation, rather than having actually to be included in it. This avoids the awkward moment which can sometimes occur as the words are actually being delivered. Here are some well-tried examples:*

**D1** 'I wonder if I dare ask for a rise?'

**D2** 'Nobody in this house understands me!'

**D3** 'I'm not having you out on the streets after dark!'

**D4** 'I'm sorry to have to tell you . . .'

**D5** 'Can you lend me a couple of quid?'

**D6** 'I always knew this would happen.'

**D7** 'Have you heard the latest . . . ?

**D8** 'I dunno, young people these days . . . they're ignorant!'

**D9** 'Now what's going on here, then – eh?'

**D10** 'I'm sorry, we didn't mean things to turn out this way.'

**D11** 'It's no good, she'll *have* to go!'

**D12** 'Why can't you do a decent day's work for a change!'

**D13** 'Excuse me, I'm new here . . .'

**D14** 'Look, I've told you, I'm not getting involved!'

**D15** 'He always was a loner, wasn't he?'

*Some examination boards simply give titles as starters for improvisations. Here are some examples to try out:*

**D16**  No Work

**D17**  The Depths of Despair

**D18**  The Factory

**D19**  Union Dispute

**D20**  Nobody Cared

**D21**  The Outsider

**D22**  A Difficult Case for Treatment

**D23**  Friend or Foe

**D24**  The Letter

**D25**  The Decision

**D26**  This House is Condemned

**D27**  Officialdom Rules Here!

**D28**  The Mistake

**D29**  The Visitor

**D30**  The Interview

*'Don't you think a sit-down strike in the Head's office is taking things a bit far?' (D19)*

*Proverbs are themselves fertile stimuli for group discussion, but try these proverbs as starters for improvisation after spending some time discussing their meaning.*

**D31**   Absence makes the heart grow fonder

**D32**   A friend in need is a friend indeed

**D33**   Better late than never

**D34**   Blood is thicker than water

**D35**   A drowning man clutches at straws

**D36**   Spare the rod: spoil the child

**D37**   A rolling stone gathers no moss

**D38**   A bird in the hand is worth two in the bush

Or these more difficult ones:

**D39**   A road may seem straightforward to a man,
yet may end as the way to death

**D40**   Better a dry crust and concord with it,
than a house full of feasting and strife

**D41**   Groups could try to invent proverbs, or wise sayings, for themselves and create improvisations around them.

*A more structured way of introducing ideas for improvisations would be for group leaders to issue each group with an information sheet on which basic material such as: setting, characters involved, situation etc, is given. Here are some examples, for small to larger groups.*

## D42   AN IMPROVISATION FOR FOUR

**SETTING**   Café
**CHARACTERS**   Four unemployed teenagers

Three of this group are sitting in the café which they visit every day because it is warm and it gives them something to do.

Establish that they are bored and unhappy and that they haven't much money. Then the fourth member of the group arrives. S/he has a bright idea to get some money and occupy their time. What is it; what happens?

## D43　AN IMPROVISATION FOR FOUR, OR MORE

**SETTING**　A family meal time
**CHARACTERS**　Members of a family

Mother and son/daughter are at home. Mother has just returned home from her full-time job to find son/daughter reading a comic/magazine instead of helping to prepare the evening meal. Older son/daughter arrives home in a hurry and is annoyed to find no meal ready, as he/she is hoping to go out later that evening to a disco. Then father arrives home, tired after a busy day at work, expecting – and looking forward to his tea. Mother becomes upset feeling she cannot cope with a full-time job and the demands of the family. Father says they need the money that mother's job provides. What argument/discussion would follow?
N.B. It is useful to have follow-up discussions after improvisations of this kind in which the assumptions of the characters presented can be challenged.

## D44　IMPROVISATION FOR FOUR, OR MORE

**SETTING**　Family sitting-room
**CHARACTERS**　Two families living next door to one another

The Allan family moved to the semi-detached house next door to the Ford family about a week ago, and on the day they moved in Mrs Ford invited them round for drinks. That evening has now arrived, but unfortunately, since moving in, the Allans have been keeping the Fords awake late at night by making noise. *You* decide the nature of that noise, and why it might be important for the Fords to get a good night's sleep. What happens when the Allans come round for a pleasant social evening, and Mr Ford mentions the question of the noise. . . ?

## D45 IMPROVISATION FOR SIX OR MORE

**SETTING**   Factory or office
**CHARACTERS**   Factory/office manager; any number of workers

The aim of this improvisation is to establish the nature and behaviour of the characters involved in it. As a minimum the improvisation should contain: someone who may be lazy or conscientious who is in charge of the office or workshop; a worker who is keen, enthusiastic and conscientious; a worker who is extremely lazy and always trying to offload work on to someone else; a gossip; someone who 'tells tales' to the management; a newcomer; several ordinary workers. Try firstly to set up a convincing working situation. Then introduce a storyline or plot. *Ideas*: one of the workers learns from the manager that they are to be made redundant; one of the workers goes to the manager to complain about something. Think of a good plot, then decide what happens.

## D46 IMPROVISATION FOR FIVE, SIX OR MORE

**SETTING**   Coin-operated laundry
**CHARACTERS**   Five or more people using the laundry

Build the improvisation gradually, having constructed a simple basic setting using chairs and tables to represent the washing machines. Start with only one or two characters present, then allow others to join in at intervals. When a convincing scene has been created, add an element of plot. *Ideas*: one of the characters returns to find his washing has been stolen; or one of the characters loses money in a machine and complains to the owner, who is unsympathetic. Or, think of something better, and decide what happens.

*Another fertile area which can act as an effective stimulus for improvisations is the quotation. Any good dictionary of quotations will provide an endless and original supply, but try these first (from* THE PENGUIN DICTIONARY OF MODERN QUOTATIONS*). They should provoke some interesting group discussion about the meaning and implications of the quotations before any attempt is made at improvising around them.*

**D47**  Human life is mainly a process of filling in time until the arrival of death
(Eric Berne, *Games People Play*)

**D48**  Money is a singular thing. It ranks with love as man's greatest source of joy. And with death as his greatest source of anxiety.
(JK Galbraith, *The Affluent Society*)

**D49**  How does it feel/ To be without a home/ Like a complete unknown/ Like a rolling stone
(Bob Dylan, *Like A Rolling Stone*)

**D50**  All the lonely people, where do they all come from?
All the lonely people, where do they all belong?
(John Lennon and Paul Macartney, *Eleanor Rigby*)

**D51**  The customer is always right.
(H Gordon Selfridge, shop slogan)

**D52**  For every person wishing to teach there are thirty not wanting to be taught.
(WC Sellar & RJ Yeatman, *1066 and All That*)

**D53**  I love mankind – it's people I can't stand
(Charles M Schulz, *Go Fly a Kite, Charlie Brown*)

*Finally, poems provide excellent stimulus material for improvisations. Not only do they provide an effective starter for talk and discussion in themselves, but they also offer interesting possibilities for improvisation. In some cases, groups working on improvisations arising out of poems have* *chosen to integrate the poetry as part of the improvisation, and have as a result, almost without realising it, produced work of a polished, theatrical quality. Whilst not wishing to stress performance as being more important than improvisation and thus enter the tedious drama-versus-theatre argument, there **is** a place for polished performance work in any educational drama course.*

*Here are some poems which have been found to be effective starters for improvisations:*

**D54** COMMUNICATION: LONELINESS
'Not Waving But Drowning' by Stevie Smith

**D55** TEENAGE REBELLION: THE PROTEST OF THE INDIVIDUAL
'Little Johnny's Confession' by Brian Patten

**D56** BIRTH: THE QUALITY OF LIFE
'The Almond Tree' by Jon Stallworthy

Poems D54–56 can be found in *British Poetry Since 1945*, Edited by Edward Lucie-Smith, Penguin, 1970

**D57** UNEMPLOYMENT
'Moving Through The Silent Crowd' by Stephen Spender

**D58** LIFE
'Prayer Before Birth' by Louis Macneice

**D59** OLD AGE
'One Flesh' by Elizabeth Jennings

**D60** SCHOOL
'The Pay is Good' by Richard Kell

**D61** SCHOOL
'The Educators' by DM Black

Poems D57–61 can be found in *Modern Poetry: A Selection*, by John Rowe Townsend, Oxford University Press, 1973.

Other effective 'starter' poems include 'Nock Nock Oo Nock E Nock' by Jimi Rand; 'Old Father' by Hugh Boatswain; 'Lonesome Walker' by Denis Watson (all from *Bluefoot Traveller*, ed. James

61

Berry, Harrap, 1981) and 'Am I O.K.?', Fran Landesman; 'Snack Bar', Stanley Cook; 'I'm no good, that's what I've been told', Roger McGough; 'Harassment', Frederick Williams; 'Love', Ian Chrichton Smith; 'First Ice', Andrey Voznesensky; 'Interview', Iain Chrichton Smith and 'The Presentation', Ripyard Cuddling (all from *Standpoints*, ed. John L Foster, Harrap, 1983).

**D62** For dozens more ideas for improvisations, this time leading out of text work, see *Themes from Life*; a sampler of contemporary drama by Graham Stoate, Harrap, 1983.

# E SUGGESTED LESSON PLANS

This section offers twenty structured lesson plans which could serve as the starting point for a drama course. Once teachers have familiarised themselves with the games and exercises contained in *Dramastarters*, they should quickly become skilful in constructing lesson strategies to suit their own teaching style and the differing needs of groups they have to teach.

The lesson plans shown here are based on the timings and aims given in the introduction. They assume little or no previous drama experience and are meant to provide a progressive strategy for secondary students, moving from fairly easy, straightforward work, to more demanding work over a number of sessions.

At the beginning, the emphasis is on games and largely physical exercises, the aim being to enable the group to get to know each other, and for their leader to begin to assess their strengths and weaknesses. Gradually, these games and exercises become fewer and at the same time more difficult and demanding, leading eventually to improvisations and larger group work. In oral as well as physical activity, the aim is to build confidence progressively, moving gradually from solo to

pair to larger group involvement. It will be noted that quite a
few sessions take place before any Section D work is attempted,
and even when this is begun, the demands made of the group
are structured and progressive.

# LESSON PLANS

**E1**  SECTION A:   A1; A2; A3; A6
     SECTION B:   B8; B17; B29;
                  B32; B33
     SECTION C:   C7; C6; C11

**E2**  SECTION A:   A6; A7
     SECTION B:   B1; B30
     SECTION C:   C1; C2; C3; C20

**E3**  SECTION A:   A11; A9; A18
     SECTION B:   B3; B6; B30
                  (briefly); B35;
                  B43
     SECTION C:   C6; C2; C12; C17

**E4**  SECTION A:   A14; A13
     SECTION B:   B2; B30
                  (briefly); B36
     SECTION C:   C18

**E5**  SECTION A:   A15; A16
     SECTION B:   B4; B42
     SECTION C:   C20

**E6**  SECTION A:   A17; A18
     SECTION B:   B6; B8
     SECTION C:   C23; C8

**E7**  SECTION A:   A8
     SECTION B:   B10; B43
     SECTION C:   C24; C25; C26

**E8**  SECTION A:   A19; A20
     SECTION B:   B12; B40; B41
     SECTION C:   C27

**E9**  SECTION A:   A21; A22; A23
     SECTION B:   B15; B16; B45
     SECTION C:   C28

**E10**  SECTION A:   A25; A24
      SECTION B:   B17; B18
      SECTION C:   C30

**E11**  SECTION A:   A28; A29; A30
      SECTION B:   B17; B18
      SECTION C:   C4; C5
      SECTION D:   D42

**E12**  SECTION A:   A32; A33;
                   A34; A35
      SECTION B:   B19
      SECTION C:   C8
      SECTION D:   D43

**E13**  SECTION A:   A36; A37
      SECTION B:   B20; B21
      SECTION C:   C10
      SECTION D:   D44

**E14**  SECTION A:   A38; A39
      SECTION B:   B22; B23; B24
      SECTION C:   C13
      SECTION D:   D45

*'I've just done a whole lesson using your knitting pattern instead of my **Dramastarters** lesson plans!'*

**E15**
SECTION A: A41
SECTION B: B25
SECTION C: C15
SECTION D: D46

**E16**
SECTION A: A42
SECTION B: B26; B27
SECTION C: C16
SECTION D: D49

**E17**
SECTION A: A44
SECTION B: B51
SECTION C: C17; C18; C19
SECTION D: D50

**E18**
SECTION A: A26
SECTION B: B52; B53; B54
SECTION C: C3
SECTION D: D19

**E19**
SECTION A: A40
SECTION B: B54
SECTION C: C4; C5
SECTION D: D26

**E20**
SECTION A: A4
SECTION B: B55; B56
SECTION C: C8
SECTION D: D54